Renaissance ART

NATIONAL GALLERY of ART
WASHINGTON

a book of postcards

Pomegranate

SAN FRANCISCO

Pomegranate Communications, Inc.
Box 808022, Petaluma CA 94975
800 227 1428; www.pomegranate.com

Pomegranate Europe Ltd.
Unit 1, Heathcote Business Centre, Hurlbutt Road
Warwick, Warwickshire CV34 6TD, UK
[+44] 0 1926 430111; sales@pomeurope.co.uk

ISBN 978-0-7649-2826-0
Pomegranate Catalog No. AA236

© 2004 National Gallery of Art, Washington

Pomegranate publishes books of
postcards on a wide range of subjects.
Please contact the publisher for more information.

Cover designed by Lisa Alban
Printed in China

16 15 14 13 12 11 10 09 08 07   11 10 9 8 7 6 5 4 3 2

To facilitate detachment of the postcards from this book, fold each card along its perforation line before tearing.

In the late Middle Ages, all of Europe favored a decorative and courtly manner known as the International Style, but by the early fifteenth century, people in Florence and other towns of central Italy believed that they were living in a new era—the Renaissance. The term "Renaissance" describes the period of "rebirth" from the dark ages of intellectual decline that followed the brilliance of ancient civilization. In Italy, especially, the Renaissance was spurred by a revival of Greek and Roman learning. Works by classical authors, lost to the West for centuries, were rediscovered, creating a new, humanistic outlook that placed human achievement at the center of all things. Not only did the Renaissance see an increase in patronage from private individuals, it also saw the introduction of new, secular subjects.

During the Renaissance, artists learned to depict the visual world in a more naturalistic manner. They extended their understanding of light and shadow, as well as space and anatomy. The idealized statuary of classical antiquity served as models for artists, while architects applied the classical orders to Renaissance buildings. Portraiture flourished during the Renaissance, as well as visual explorations of the pastoral landscape.

Renaissance ART

Fra Angelico (Florentine, c. 1395–1455)
and Filippo Lippi (Florentine, c. 1406–1469)
The Adoration of the Magi, c. 1445
Tempera on panel, diameter: 137.3 cm
National Gallery of Art, Washington
Samuel H. Kress Collection 1952.2.2

BOX 808022   PETALUMA   CA 94975

Pomegranate

© National Gallery of Art, Washington

Renaissance
ART

Giovanni Bellini (Venetian, c. 1430/1435–1516)
Orpheus, c. 1515
Oil on panel transferred to canvas, 39.5 x 81 cm
National Gallery of Art, Washington
Widener Collection 1942.9.2

Pomegranate

BOX 808022   PETALUMA   CA 94975

© National Gallery of Art, Washington

Renaissance
ART

Giovanni Bellini (Venetian, c. 1430/1435–1516)
Portrait of a Young Man in Red, c. 1480
Oil and tempera on panel, 32 x 26.5 cm
National Gallery of Art, Washington
Andrew W. Mellon Collection 1937.1.29

Pomegranate

BOX 808022   PETALUMA   CA 94975

© National Gallery of Art, Washington

Renaissance
ART

Giovanni Bellini (Venetian, c. 1430/1435–1516)
and Titian (Venetian, c. 1490–1576)
The Feast of the Gods, 1514/1529
Oil on canvas, 170.2 x 188 cm
National Gallery of Art, Washington
Widener Collection 1942.9.1

Pomegranate   BOX 808022   PETALUMA   CA 94975

© National Gallery of Art, Washington

Renaissance
ART

Botticelli (Florentine, 1446–1510)
The Adoration of the Magi, early 1480s
Tempera and oil on panel, 68 x 102 cm
National Gallery of Art, Washington
Andrew W. Mellon Collection 1937.1.22

BOX 808022 PETALUMA CA 94975

Pomegranate

© National Gallery of Art, Washington

Renaissance
ART

Botticelli (Florentine, 1446–1510)
Portrait of a Youth, early 1480s
Tempera on panel, 41.7 x 30.9 cm
National Gallery of Art, Washington
Andrew W. Mellon Collection 1937.1.19

Pomegranate   BOX 808022   PETALUMA   CA 94975

© National Gallery of Art, Washington

Renaissance
ART

Agnolo Bronzino (Florentine, 1503–1572)
A Young Woman and Her Little Boy, c. 1540
Oil on panel, 99.5 x 76 cm
National Gallery of Art, Washington
Widener Collection 1942.9.6

BOX 808022 PETALUMA CA 94975

Pomegranate

© National Gallery of Art, Washington

Renaissance
ART

Vittore Carpaccio (Venetian, c. 1465–1525/1526)
The Virgin Reading, c. 1505
Oil on panel transferred to canvas, 78 x 51 cm
National Gallery of Art, Washington
Samuel H. Kress Collection 1939.1.354

BOX 808022   PETALUMA   CA 94975

Pomegranate

© National Gallery of Art, Washington

Renaissance
ART

Biagio d'Antonio (Florentine, c. 1446–1516)
Portrait of a Boy, probably 1475/1480
Oil and tempera on panel, 41.9 x 35.9 cm
National Gallery of Art, Washington
Samuel H. Kress Collection 1939.1.179

BOX 808022   PETALUMA   CA 94975

Pomegranate

© National Gallery of Art, Washington

Renaissance
ART

Masolino da Panicale (Florentine, c. 1383–1435 or after)
The Archangel Gabriel, probably 1420/1430
Tempera on panel, 76.6 x 57.8 cm
National Gallery of Art, Washington
Samuel H. Kress Collection 1939.1.225

BOX 808022   PETALUMA   CA 94975

Pomegranate

© National Gallery of Art, Washington

Renaissance
ART

Leonardo da Vinci (Florentine, 1452–1519)
Ginevra de' Benci, obverse, c. 1474
Oil on panel, 38.1 x 37 cm
National Gallery of Art, Washington
Ailsa Mellon Bruce Fund 1967.6.1.a

Pomegranate

BOX 808022   PETALUMA   CA 94975

© National Gallery of Art, Washington

Renaissance
ART

Gerard David (Bruges, c. 1460–1523)
The Rest on the Flight into Egypt, c. 1510
Oil on panel, 41.9 x 42.2 cm
National Gallery of Art, Washington
Andrew W. Mellon Collection 1937.1.43

BOX 808022   PETALUMA   CA 94975

Pomegranate

© National Gallery of Art, Washington

Sebastiano del Piombo (Venetian, 1485–1547)
Cardinal Bandinello Sauli, His Secretary, and Two Geographers, 1516
Oil on panel transferred to canvas, 121.8 x 150.4 cm
National Gallery of Art, Washington
Samuel H. Kress Collection 1961.9.37

BOX 808022   PETALUMA   CA 94975

Pomegranate

© National Gallery of Art, Washington

Renaissance
ART

Albrecht Dürer (German, 1471–1528)
Lot and His Daughters, reverse, c. 1496/1499
Oil on panel, 52.4 x 42.2 cm
National Gallery of Art, Washington
Samuel H. Kress Collection 1952.2.16.b

BOX 808022   PETALUMA   CA 94975

Pomegranate

© National Gallery of Art, Washington

Renaissance
ART

Albrecht Dürer (German, 1471–1528)
Portrait of a Clergyman (Johann Dorsch?), 1516
Oil on parchment on fabric, 41.7 x 32.7 cm
National Gallery of Art, Washington
Samuel H. Kress Collection 1952.2.17

Pomegranate

BOX 808022   PETALUMA   CA 94975

© National Gallery of Art, Washington

Renaissance
ART

Fra Angelico (Florentine, c. 1395–1455)
The Healing of Palladia by Saint Cosmas and Saint Damian,
probably 1438/1443
Tempera (and oil?) on panel, 36.2 x 46.3 cm
National Gallery of Art, Washington
Samuel H. Kress Collection 1952.5.3

BOX 808022 PETALUMA CA 94975

Pomegranate

© National Gallery of Art, Washington

Renaissance
ART

Filippo Lippi (Florentine, c. 1406–1469)
Madonna and Child, 1440/1445
Tempera on panel, 79 x 51.1 cm
National Gallery of Art, Washington
Samuel H. Kress Collection 1939.1.290

BOX 808022   PETALUMA   CA 94975

Pomegranate

© National Gallery of Art, Washington

Renaissance
ART

Filippino Lippi (Florentine, 1457–1504)
Tobias and the Angel, probably c. 1480
Oil and tempera (?) on panel, 32.7 x 23.5 cm
National Gallery of Art, Washington
Samuel H. Kress Collection 1939.1.229

BOX 808022   PETALUMA   CA 94975

Pomegranate

© National Gallery of Art, Washington

Renaissance
ART

Lorenzo Lotto (Venetian, c. 1480–1556/1557)
Saint Catherine, 1522
Oil on panel, 57.2 x 50.2 cm
National Gallery of Art, Washington
Samuel H. Kress Collection 1939.1.117

Pomegranate

BOX 808022   PETALUMA   CA 94975

© National Gallery of Art, Washington

Renaissance
ART

Lucas Cranach the Elder (German, 1472–1553)
A Princess of Saxony, c. 1517
Oil on panel, 43.4 x 34.3 cm
National Gallery of Art, Washington
Ralph and Mary Booth Collection 1947.6.2

BOX 808022   PETALUMA   CA 94975

Pomegranate

© National Gallery of Art, Washington

Renaissance
ART

Bernardino Luini (Milanese, c. 1480–1532)
Portrait of a Lady, 1520/1525
Oil on panel, 77 x 57.5 cm
National Gallery of Art, Washington
Andrew W. Mellon Collection 1937.1.37

BOX 808022   PETALUMA   CA 94975

Pomegranate

© National Gallery of Art, Washington

Renaissance ART

Hans Memling (Bruges, active c. 1465–1494)
Madonna and Child with Angels, after 1479
Oil on panel, 57.6 x 46.4 cm
National Gallery of Art, Washington
Andrew W. Mellon Collection 1937.1.41

Pomegranate

BOX 808022   PETALUMA   CA 94975

© National Gallery of Art, Washington

Renaissance
ART

Raphael (Central Italian, 1483–1520)
Bindo Altoviti, c. 1515
Oil on panel, 59.7 x 43.8 cm
National Gallery of Art, Washington
Samuel H. Kress Collection 1943.4.33

Pomegranate BOX 808022 PETALUMA CA 94975

© National Gallery of Art, Washington

Renaissance
ART

Raphael (Central Italian, 1483–1520)
Saint George and the Dragon, c. 1506
Oil on panel, 28.5 x 21.5 cm
National Gallery of Art, Washington
Andrew W. Mellon Collection 1937.1.26

BOX 808022   PETALUMA   CA 94975

Pomegranate

© National Gallery of Art, Washington

Renaissance
ART

Jacopo Bassano (Venetian, c. 1510–1592)
The Miraculous Draught of Fishes, 1545
Oil on canvas, 143.5 x 243.7 cm
National Gallery of Art, Washington
Patrons' Permanent Fund 1997.21.1

BOX 808022   PETALUMA   CA 94975

Pomegranate

© National Gallery of Art, Washington

Renaissance
ART

Raphael (Central Italian, 1483–1520)
The Small Cowper Madonna, c. 1505
Oil on panel, 59.5 x 44 cm
National Gallery of Art, Washington
Widener Collection 1942.9.57

Pomegranate   BOX 808022   PETALUMA   CA 94975

© National Gallery of Art, Washington

Renaissance
ART

Titian (Venetian, c. 1490–1576)
Doge Andrea Gritti, 1546–1548
Oil on canvas, 133.6 x 103.2 cm
National Gallery of Art, Washington
Samuel H. Kress Collection 1961.9.45

Pomegranate

BOX 808022   PETALUMA   CA 94975

© National Gallery of Art, Washington

Renaissance
ART

Titian (Venetian, c. 1490–1576)
Portrait of a Lady, c. 1555
Oil on canvas, 97.8 x 74 cm
National Gallery of Art, Washington
Samuel H. Kress Collection 1939.1.292

BOX 808022   PETALUMA   CA 94975

Pomegranate

© National Gallery of Art, Washington

Renaissance
ART

Rogier van der Weyden
(Netherlandish, 1399/1400–1464)
Portrait of a Lady, c. 1460
Oil on panel, 34 x 25.5 cm
National Gallery of Art, Washington
Andrew W. Mellon Collection 1937.1.44

BOX 808022 PETALUMA CA 94975

Pomegranate

© National Gallery of Art, Washington

Renaissance
ART

Jan van Eyck (Netherlandish, c. 1390–1441)
The Annunciation, c. 1434/1436
Oil on canvas transferred from panel, 90.2 x 34.1 cm
National Gallery of Art, Washington
Andrew W. Mellon Collection 1937.1.39

BOX 808022   PETALUMA   CA 94975

Pomegranate

© National Gallery of Art, Washington